JOHN THOMPSON'S
EASIEST PIANO COURSE

FIRST WORSHIP SONGS

ISBN 978-1-61774-327-6

EXCLUSIVELY DISTRIBUTED BY

HAL•LEONARD®
CORPORATION
7777 W. BLUEMOUND RD. P.O. BOX 13819
MILWAUKEE, WISCONSIN 53213

Visit Hal Leonard Online at
www.halleonard.com

Teachers and Parents

This collection of worship songs, arranged in the John Thompson tradition,
is intended as supplementary material for the elementary level pianist. The pieces may also be
used for sight-reading practice by more advanced students.

CONTENTS

More Precious Than Silver

Words and Music by Lynn DeShazo
Arranged by Glenda Austin

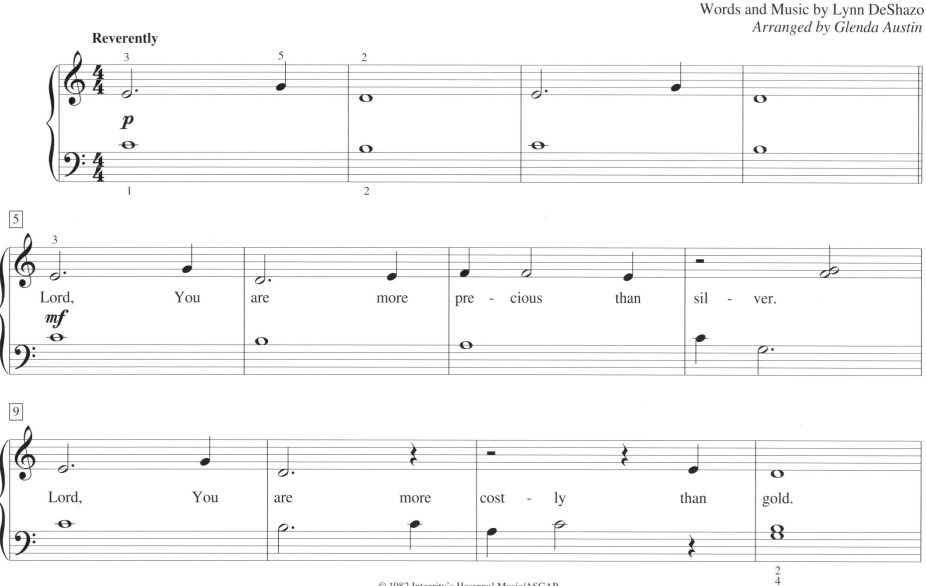

Lord, You are more pre - cious than sil - ver.

Lord, You are more cost - ly than gold.

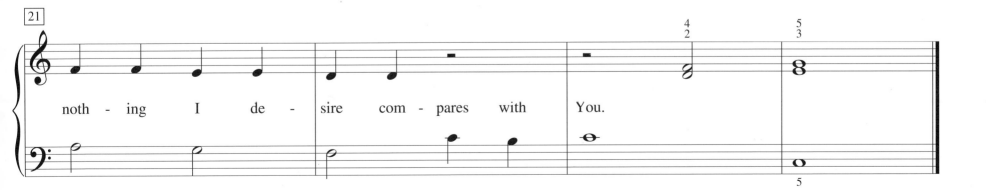

Your Grace Is Enough

Words and Music by Matt Maher
Arranged by Glenda Austin

Awesome God

Words and Music by Rich Mullins
Arranged by Glenda Austin

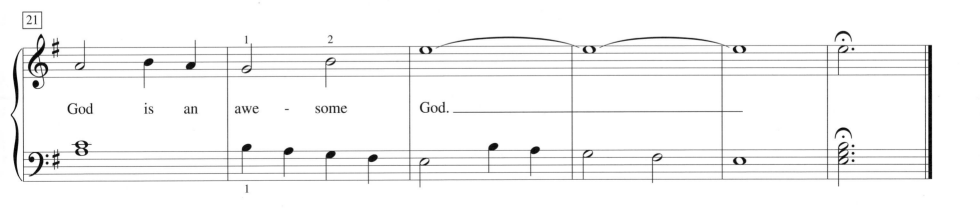

There Is a Redeemer

Words and Music by Melody Green
Arranged by Glenda Austin

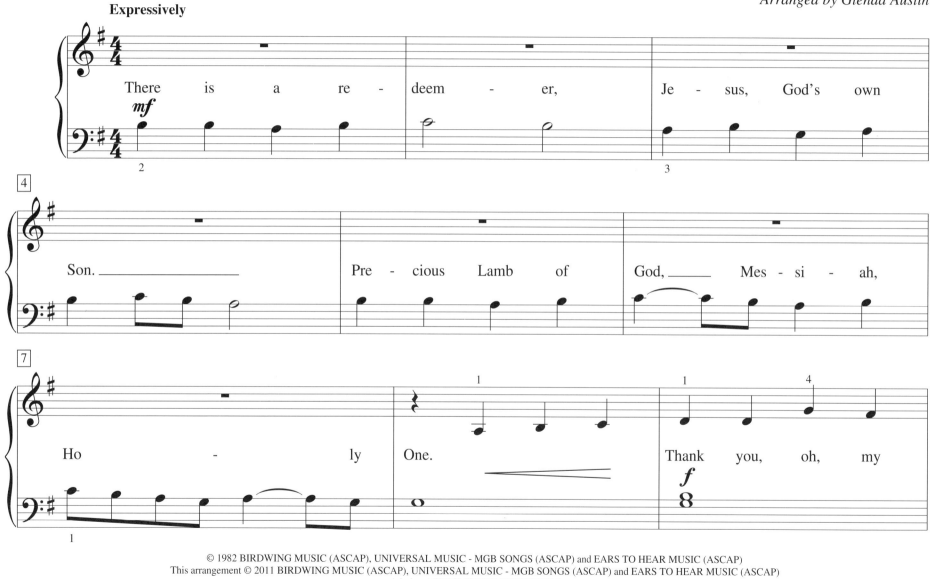

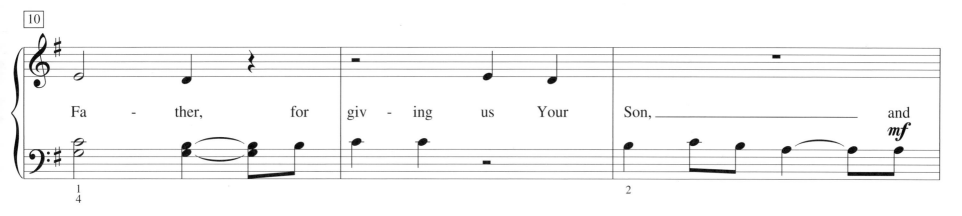

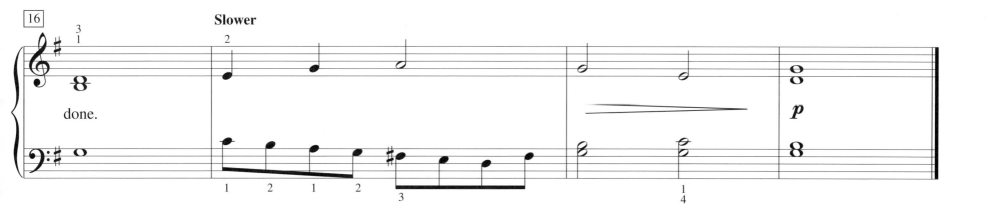

Hosanna
(Praise Is Rising)

Words and Music by Paul Baloche and Brenton Brown
Arranged by Glenda Austin

13

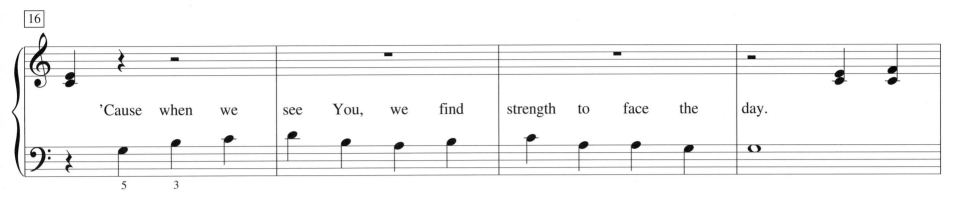

'Cause when we see You, we find strength to face the day.

In Your pres - ence, all our fears are washed a - way, washed a -

way. Ho - san - na, ho - san -

Here I Am to Worship

Words and Music by Tim Hughes
Arranged by Glenda Austin

17

Thy Word

Words and Music by Michael W. Smith and Amy Grant
Arranged by Glenda Austin

With confidence

Praise the Name of Jesus

Words and Music by Roy Hicks, Jr.
Arranged by Glenda Austin

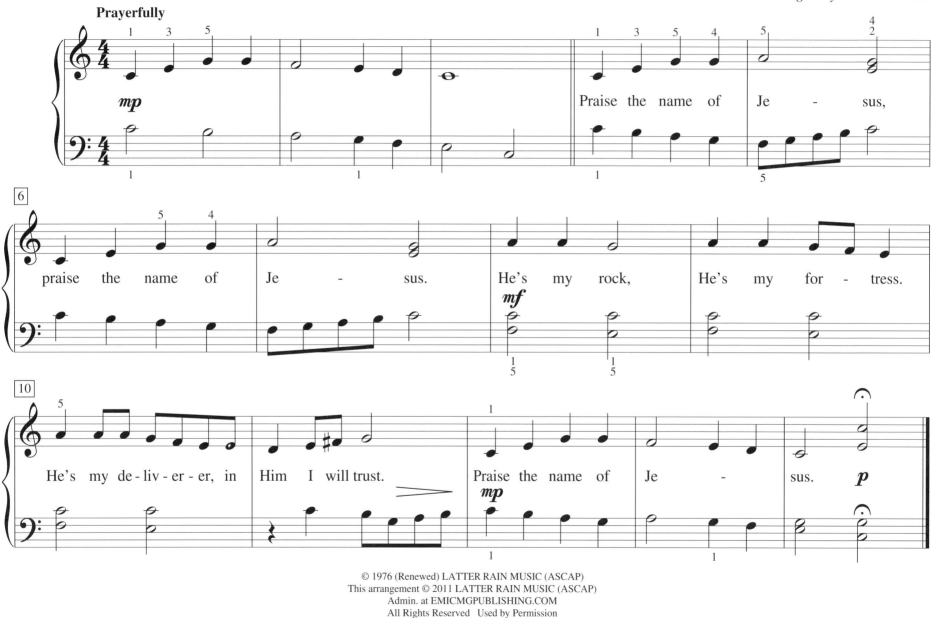

TEACHING LITTLE FINGERS TO PLAY

TEACHING LITTLE FINGERS TO PLAY

by John Thompson

A series for the early beginner combining rote and note approach. The melodies are written with careful thought and are kept as simple as possible, yet they are refreshingly delightful. All the music lies within the grasp of the child's small hands.

00412076　Book only $6.99
00406523　Book/Audio...$9.99

TEACHING LITTLE FINGERS TO PLAY ENSEMBLE

by John Thompson

A book of intermediate-level accompaniments for use in the teacher's studio or at home. Two possible accompaniments are included for each *Teaching Little Fingers* piece: a Secondo or Primo part, as well as a second piano part for studios that have two pianos/keyboards.

00412228　Book only $5.99

DISNEY TUNES

arr. Glenda Austin

10 delightful Disney songs: The Bare Necessities • Can You Feel the Love Tonight • Candle on the Water • God Help the Outcasts • Kiss the Girl • Mickey Mouse March • The Siamese Cat Song • Winnie the Pooh • You'll Be in My Heart (Pop Version) • Zip-A-Dee-Doo-Dah.

00416748　Book only $9.99
00416749　Book/Audio...$12.99

CHRISTMAS CAROLS

arr. Carolyn Miller

12 piano solos: Angels We Have Heard on High • Deck the Hall • The First Noel • Hark! The Herald Angels Sing • Jingle Bells • Jolly Old Saint Nicholas • Joy to the World! • O Come, All Ye Faithful • O Come Little Children • Silent Night • Up on the Housetop • We Three Kings of Orient Are.

00406391　Book only $6.99
00406722　Book/Audio...$10.99

CLASSICS

arr. Randall Hartsell

11 piano classics: Bridal Chorus (from *Lohengrin*) (Wagner) • Can-Can (from *Orpheus in the Underworld*) (Offenbach) • Country Gardens (English Folk Tune) • A Little Night Music (from *Eine kleine Nachtmusik*) (Mozart) • Lullaby (Brahms) • Ode to Joy (from Symphony No. 9) (Beethoven) • Symphony No. 5 (Second Movement) (Tchaikovsky) • and more.

00406550　Book only $6.99
00406736　Book/Audio...$10.99

HYMNS

arr. Mary K. Sallee

11 hymns: Amazing Grace • Faith of Our Fathers • For the Beauty of the Earth • Holy, Holy, Holy • Jesus Loves Me • Jesus Loves the Little Children • Joyful, Joyful, We Adore Thee • Kum Bah Yah • Praise Him, All Ye Little Children • We Are Climbing Jacob's Ladder • What a Friend We Have in Jesus.

00406413　Book only $6.99
00406731　Book/Audio...$10.99

TEACHING LITTLE FINGERS TO PLAY MORE

by Leigh Kaplan

Teaching Little Fingers to Play More is a fun-filled and colorfully illustrated follow-up book to *Teaching Little Fingers to Play*. This book strengthens skills learned while easing the transition into John Thompson's *Modern Course, Book One*.

00406137　Book only $6.99
00406527　Book/Audio...$9.99

MORE DISNEY TUNES

arr. Glenda Austin

9 songs, including: Circle of Life • Colors of the Wind • A Dream Is a Wish Your Heart Makes • A Spoonful of Sugar • Under the Sea • A Whole New World • and more.

00416750　Book only $9.99
00416751　Book/Audio...$12.99

MORE EASY DUETS

arr. Carolyn Miller

9 more fun duets arranged for 1 piano, 4 hands: A Bicycle Built for Two (Daisy Bell) • Blow the Man Down • Chopsticks • Do Your Ears Hang Low? • I've Been Working on the Railroad • The Man on the Flying Trapeze • Short'nin' Bread • Skip to My Lou • The Yellow Rose of Texas.

00416832　Book only $6.99
00416833　Book/Audio...$10.99

MORE BROADWAY SONGS

arr. Carolyn Miller

10 more fantastic Broadway favorites arranged for a young performer, including: Castle on a Cloud • Climb Ev'ry Mountain • Gary, Indiana • In My Own Little Corner • It's the Hard-Knock Life • Memory • Oh, What a Beautiful Mornin' • Sunrise, Sunset • Think of Me • Where Is Love?

00416928　Book only $6.99
00416929　Book/Audio...$12.99

MORE CHILDREN'S SONGS

arr. by Carolyn Miller

10 songs: The Candy Man • Do-Re-Mi • I'm Popeye the Sailor Man • It's a Small World • Linus and Lucy • The Muppet Show Theme • My Favorite Things • Sesame Street Theme • Supercalifragilisticexpialidocious • Tomorrow.

00416810　Book only $6.99
00416811　Book/Audio...$12.99

EXCLUSIVELY DISTRIBUTED BY

WILLIS MUSIC

HAL•LEONARD®
CORPORATION
7777 W. BLUEMOUND RD. P.O. BOX 13819
MILWAUKEE, WISCONSIN 53213

Prices, contents, and availability subject to change without notice.
Disney characters and artwork © Disney Enterprises, Inc.

All arrangements come with optional teacher accompaniments.

FOR A COMPLETE SERIES LISTING, VISIT WWW.HALLEONARD.COM

0617

JOHN THOMPSON'S
EASIEST PIANO COURSE

Fun repertoire books are available as an integral part of **John Thompson's Easiest Piano Course**. Graded to work alongside the course, these pieces are ideal for pupils reaching the end of Part 2. They are invaluable for securing basic technique as well as developing musicality and enjoyment.

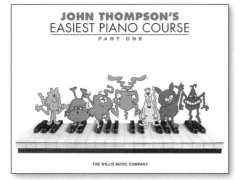

John Thompson's Easiest Piano Course

00414014 Part 1 – Book only $6.99
00414018 Part 2 – Book only $6.99
00414019 Part 3 – Book only $6.99
00414112 Part 4 – Book only $6.99

First Pop Songs *arr. Miller*

00416954 .... $8.99

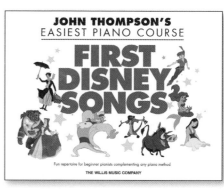

First Classics

00406347 .... $6.99

First Disney Songs *arr. Miller*

00416880 .... $9.99

First Jazz Tunes *arr. Baumgartner*

00120872 .... $7.99

First Beethoven *arr. Hussey*

00171709 .... $7.99

First Chart Hits

00141171 .... $7.99

Also available:

First Mozart *arr. Hussey*
00171851 .... $7.99

First Nursery Rhymes
00406229 .... $6.99

First Worship Songs *arr. Austin*
00416892 .... $8.99

WILLIS MUSIC

EXCLUSIVELY DISTRIBUTED BY
HAL•LEONARD®

Prices, contents and availability subject to change without notice.   Disney characters and artwork © Disney Enterprises Inc.   View complete songlists on **www.halleonard.com**